Pets and Animal Friends!

By Vanessa Mitchell

Pictures by Caroline Baum

Gareth Stevens Publishing
Milwaukee

BRIGHT IDEA BOOKS:

First Words!
Picture Dictionary!
Opposites!
Sounds!

The Four Seasons!
Pets and Animal Friends!
The Age of Dinosaurs!
Baby Animals!

Mouse Count!
Time!
Animal 1*2*3!
Animal ABC!

Homes Then and Now!
Other People, Other Homes!

Library of Congress Cataloging-in-Publication Data

Mitchell, Vanessa.
    Pets and animal friends!

    (Bright idea books)
    Bibliography: p.
    Includes index.
    Summary: Introduces animals to be found at home, in the garden, at the zoo, or on a farm, and offers suggestions for learning more about animals as friends.
    1. Pets-–Juvenile literature. 2. Animals—Juvenile literature. [1. Pets. 2. Animals] I. Baum, Caroline, ill. II. Title.
SF416.2.M58 1985   636   85-26227
ISBN 0-918831-66-0
ISBN 0-918831-65-2 (lib. bdg.)

This North American edition first published in 1985 by

Gareth Stevens, Inc.
7221 West Green Tree Road   Milwaukee, Wisconsin 53223, USA

U.S. edition, this format, copyright © 1985
Supplementary text copyright © 1985 by Gareth Stevens, Inc.
Illustrations copyright © 1984 by Octopus Books Limited

First published in the United Kingdom with an original text copyright by Octopus Books Limited.

Typeset by Ries Graphics, Ltd.
Series Editors: MaryLee Knowlton and Mark J. Sachner
Cover Design: Gary Moseley
Reading Consultant: Kathleen A. Brau

Contents

*Puppies

A puppy will become a
wonderful friend if you
take care of it. You must
feed it and groom it.
And you should play
with it and teach it
how to behave.

A large cardboard box
lined with newspapers
makes a fine bed for a
puppy.

Puppies need something to chew, like hard rubber toys or big bones. Many puppies love old slippers!

A puppy needs milk, water, and four small meals a day. Housebreak it by taking it outside after every meal.

Kittens

Kittens are lovable pets! When they are very young, they need lots of care and attention. As they grow up, they become braver and spend more time by themselves.

You can make a warm bed for your new kitten from a big cardboard box lined with soft old clothes. Your kitten will need four small meals a day and plenty of water.

You should keep your kitten indoors for the first two weeks. If you let it go outside too early, it might get lost. Once it knows your home, it can find its way back when it goes out.

*Kittens love to play! And all they need is a simple toy. A spool tied to some string will keep your kitten happy for hours.

Rabbits

Rabbits are lively pets
and need lots of
exercise. A special pen
in your yard will give
your rabbit a safe place
to run around in.

It will also need
a strong wooden
hutch to live in. Put hay in one part
for a sleeping area. Once a week,
clean out the hutch and put in
new hay.

✲If you talk to your rabbit and pet it, it will soon become tame and enjoy your company.

✲Your rabbit must be fed every morning and evening. Rabbits eat hay and cereals, such as crushed oats, wheat, and barley. They also eat vegetables such as lettuce, cabbages, carrots, and celery. And they need water every day.

Ponies

Ponies make good friends and wonderful pets.

✻Ponies like being outside in a fenced yard. The yard should have enough space for the pony to run, and grass for it to eat.

Besides grass, ponies eat bran and oats. In winter, when there's no grass, they also need hay. They should have lots of fresh water to drink all year round.

*Ride your pony every day if you can, and brush it regularly. Clean its hooves often and check to be sure its shoes are not worn or loose.

*Your pony will enjoy lots of patting and stroking. And don't forget special treats like carrots and apples!

11

Mice

Siamese

Tan

Marked

Self (gray)

White

✳Mice come in many colors. They are easily tamed and they make friendly pets.

✳Mice need a strong cage they can't chew through. They like to run around and climb onto ladders, ropes, exercise wheels, and ledges.

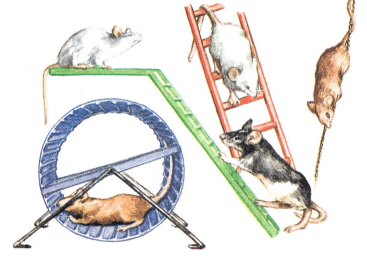

Give your mice a nesting box to sleep in and some hay or soft paper for bedding. Change the bedding once a week.

* Mice eat grains, whole-wheat bread soaked in milk, and lettuce. For a treat, give them apples, cheese, or carrots.

Gerbils

*Gerbils are clean, busy, and fun! They love to climb and jump and make burrows. The best home for them is a large glass tank with plenty of peat and straw in it. You can watch them burrowing in the peat!

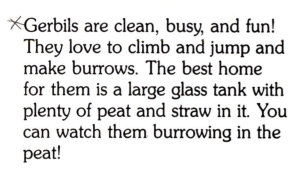

Gerbils become tame quickly and can play outside their tank. But don't let them get too tired or run away through open doors or windows. They like to play with bags, boxes, and tubes.

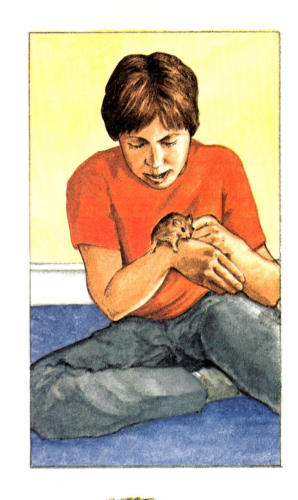

✳ Gerbils eat grains, sunflower seeds, and cornflakes. They also like apples, carrots, and lettuce.

Canaries

*Canaries are beautiful little birds. They come in yellow and many other colors, too. They are very cheerful, and they sing beautifully.

Border

Pink Gloster

Cinnamon

Frilled

Lizard

White

*Canaries like company, so you might want to get more than one!

Put twigs and swings in their cage for them to perch on. Feed them canary seed from the pet shop and give them cabbage and lettuce. The pet shop can also sell you grit to help them digest their food.

✳Keep their cage clean and make sure it is not in direct sunlight or cold air.

Parrots

✳Parrots are friendly and noisy birds! There are many kinds, and each one comes in a different size and color.

African Gray

Lutino
Cockatiel

South
American

Senegal

African Grays are favorites because they are good at copying sounds and words.

18

✳Parrots eat fruit, such as dates, apples, and oranges. They also eat parrot food, which you can buy at a pet shop.

Parrots are messy eaters! A sliding tray on the floor of their cage will make it easier to remove the food they drop. The tray will also help you keep the cage clean.

✳Parrots need lots of company. The more people they talk to, the happier they are!

If you buy a young parrot and teach it to talk, it will make an interesting and amusing pet. But make sure you really want to keep a parrot, because they can live for a long time. Some live as long as fifty years!

Turtles

*Several kinds of turtles can be kept as pets. Each kind has different shapes and colors on its skin and shell. Turtles from warm countries are kept in a glass tank.

The turtle's tank should have a heater to keep the water warm. A lamp on top of the tank will also help to keep the air warm. Turtles like to come out of the water to rest on a smooth rock under the lamp.

✳Turtles eat underwater. Here is a good way to feed them: take them out of their tank and put them in a separate feeding bowl to feed. If you put food in their tank, it will make the water dirty. Turtles eat dried insects, raw meat and fish, and green leaves.

Frogs and Toads

Frogs and toads live partly in water and partly on land. They lay their eggs, which are called spawn, in water. The eggs are covered with clear jelly, which tastes horrible to fish!

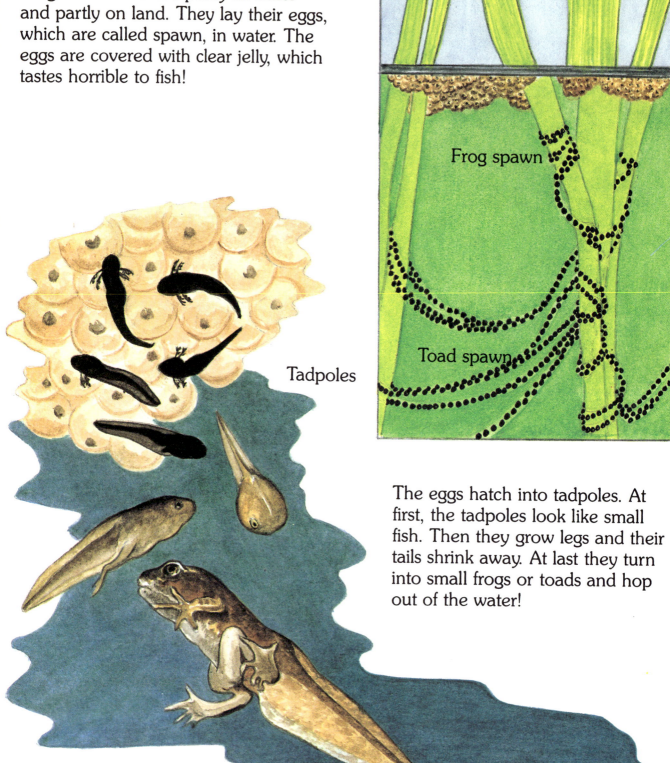

Frog spawn

Toad spawn

Tadpoles

The eggs hatch into tadpoles. At first, the tadpoles look like small fish. Then they grow legs and their tails shrink away. At last they turn into small frogs or toads and hop out of the water!

You can collect some frog or toad spawn from a pond and watch the tadpoles grow in a tank at home. Give them underwater plants to eat when they are small. As they grow bigger, give them pieces of raw meat. When they are fully grown, take them back to their pond.

Toad

Frog

Newts and Salamanders

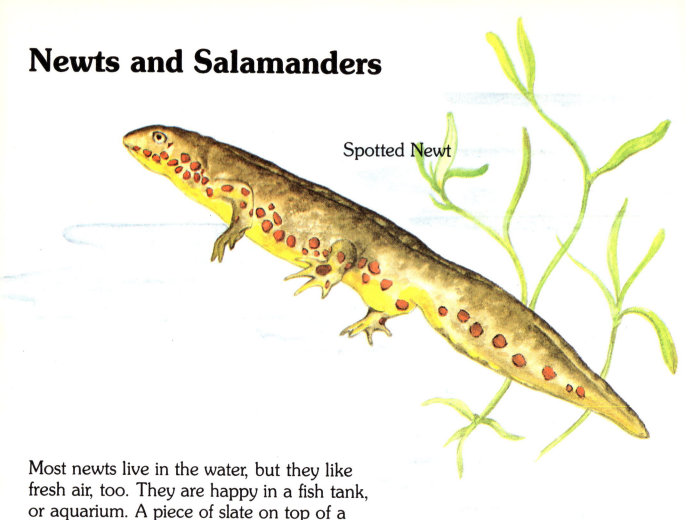

Spotted Newt

Most newts live in the water, but they like fresh air, too. They are happy in a fish tank, or aquarium. A piece of slate on top of a flower pot will give them a resting place.

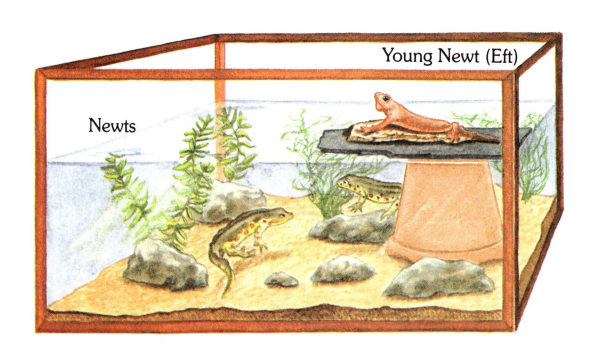

Young Newt (Eft)

Newts

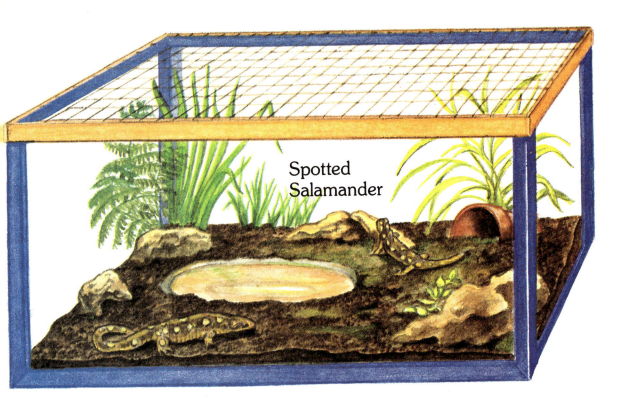

Spotted
Salamander

Salamanders like damp, shady places.
Make them a home in a glass tank. Start
with soil, moss, and peat. Then sink a
shallow dish of water in the dirt for a pond.
Add leafy plants and bark for them to hide
under.

Newts and salamanders
eat earthworms and
insects.

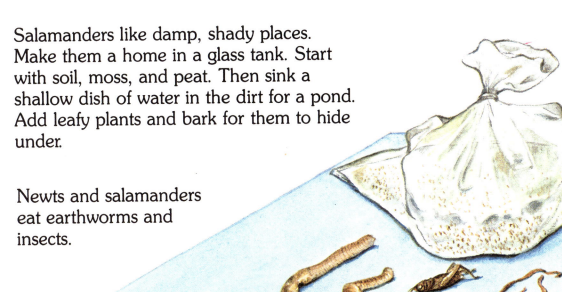

Fish

✗See how gracefully fish swim in their tank! Be sure their water is clean and well-lit. Tropical fish need a water heater to keep the water warm.

Goldfish and tropical fish come in many shapes and colors. Ask your pet shop which fish are safe to put into the same tank!

Here is how to prepare your fish tank: First put a few inches of gravel in the bottom. Then cover the gravel with paper. Now pour the water in, and the gravel will not be disturbed.

Take out the paper when the tank is full, and put some plants into the gravel.

*Fish eat mainly dried food. Sprinkle a little food on the water several times a day. Remove any food the fish do not eat at once. This will help keep the water clean.

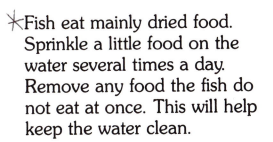

Ants

Ants are fun to watch! You will need a wood and glass ant tank. Fill it with earth and put some ants into it. Some gauze will keep them inside.

Keep the tank dark under a cloth for a day or two. Feed the ants bits of cheese, meat, and hardboiled egg. Soon you will see the tunnels and rooms they have made in the earth. See how busy they are as they lay eggs, store food, and look after the young ants!

When you have finished watching your ants, put them back where you found them outdoors.

Praying Mantises

Mantises look as if they are praying. But they are very fierce insects! They eat grasshoppers, crickets, and butterflies — and sometimes even other mantises!

Wild Birds

Wild birds may visit your yard if you put out scraps and birdseed. They come to feed more often in winter, when worms, seeds, and berries are hard to find. Give them a raised table that is high enough to keep away dogs and cats.

Starlings and sparrows are bold, noisy birds! Thrushes are shy and quiet, and the little wren with its tipped-up tail is even shyer. It will be a special time when you spot one feeding in your yard!

Starling

Sparrows

Wren

Thrush

Squirrels, Moles, and Foxes

Squirrels are frisky, bushy-tailed garden visitors. Their homes are in trees — either in a hole or in an untidy nest of twigs. They enjoy nuts, which they store for the winter.

les are night-time visitors. They dig nnels underground. They eat the rms they find and push up piles of il to the surface of the ground. They t dead leaves and twigs inside these lehills to make a cozy nest.

Foxes sometimes visit gardens to look for food. You may spot their oval-shaped footprints — especially near garbage cans!

Calves, Lambs, and Kids

Calves, lambs, and kids are baby animals. They can stand up on their wobbly legs very soon after they are born. Their mothers lick them. This is to clean them, warm them, and encourage them to feed.

Calf

They suck milk from their mothers when they are young. The mother's milk helps them grow and protects them against disease.

Kid

They love to run and jump around once they are bold enough to leave their mother's side. They are especially interested in things that move. But if anything startles them they quickly run back to their mother!

Lamb

Chicks and Piglets

These little chicks pecked their way out of their shells a few days ago. They scurry around their mother, peeping away. She clucks at them and shows them worms and grains to eat. Their father, the rooster, seems very proud, but he doesn't seem to do much!

Seven squealing piglets are hungrily sucking milk from their mother. She lies on her side so they can all reach her easily. When the piglets grow older, they feed from a trough.

Lions and Tigers

In the wild, lions and tigers are
hunters, and they roam large
areas of land. They hunt
animals such as antelopes,
zebras, and buffaloes.

They have coats of fur which help them hide
in their surroundings. The tiger's stripes look like
shadows in the grass. The lion's color matches the
sandy places where it lives.

In zoos, zoo keepers feed
the lions and tigers. They are
usually kept in large areas so
they can move around.

Elephants and Chimpanzees

Elephants are the largest and strongest of all land animals. There are two kinds: the African elephant and the Indian elephant. The African elephant is larger and has bigger ears. Elephants look fierce. They are usually gentle, however, and they do not eat meat. In zoos, elephants sometimes give rides to children.

Chimpanzees look like humans and often act like humans! They are very funny to watch. The chimpanzees' tea party is a favorite event in some zoos.

Seals and Penguins

In the wild, seals and penguins spend lots of time hunting fish.

Seals have smooth, round bodies that move fast underwater. They are friendly and smart, and they can do many tricks. Feeding time is fun to watch! They jump and dive for the fish thrown by their keeper.

Penguins are also fun to watch. On land, they waddle along awkwardly. But when they are underwater, they are very active and swim quickly. They are actually very graceful!

The following "Things to Talk About," "Things to Do," and "Index of Animal Names" sections offer grown-ups suggestions for further activities and ideas for young readers of *Pets and Animal Friends!*

Things to Talk About

1. What animal would you like most to have for a pet? Why? Which would you not want? Why not?

2. Are there any animals your parents would *not* let you have? Why?

3. Do you think any of the farm animals would make a good pet? Where would you keep it?

4. If you had a dog of your own, what would you like to do with it?

5. What would you do with each of these animals if you had one of your own:
   • a kitten?
   • a pony?
   • a fish?
   • a gerbil?

6. Can you think of any animals not in this book that would make a good pet?

7. On page 34, we see that calves, lambs, and kids are baby animals. Can you give the names for them when they become grown-up animals?

Things to Do

1. Write a short report about a day in the life of a puppy, or a kitten, or a rabbit. You may want to find some more books from the list of books on page 47. You may also want to watch a puppy, kitten, or rabbit you know.

2. Go to the zoo, if one is near you. Choose an animal that interests you, and find out how this animal lives in the wild.

3. Invite a pet store owner to your class to tell you and your classmates about good pets and how to care for them.

4. Arrange for your family or class to visit a farm or ranch. Or, if you know someone who lives or works on a farm, invite him or her to your class.

   Ask these questions about the animals raised there:

   • How much does it cost to keep them?
   • What do they do there?
   • Are they pets or are they for making money?

5. For one hour, sit outside your house or in a park, or wherever animals live. Make a list of every animal you see and what it does.

   Ask a friend who lives somewhere else to make a list, too. Compare your list with his or hers. How are they different or the same? Why?

Index of Animal Names

More Books About Pets and Animal Friends

Here are some more books about pets and animal friends. Look at the list. If you see any books you would like to read, see if your library or bookstore has them.

About Animals. Scarry (Golden Press)
The Animals of Buttercup Farm. Dunn (Random House)
Baby Animals! Thomson (Gareth Stevens)
Diary of a Rabbit. Hess (Scribner's)
The Four Seasons! Thomson (Gareth Stevens)
Frosty: A Raccoon To Remember. Weaver (Publishers Weekly)
How Kittens Grow. Selsam (Scholastic Book Service)
How Puppies Grow. Selsam (Scholastic Book Service)
Hurry Home, Candy. DeJong (Harper & Row)
Just a Dog. Griffiths (Pocket Books)
Keeping Barney. Haas (Scholastic Book Service)
Kids' Pet Book. Barrett and Dalton (Nitty Gritty Productions)
Last Puppy. Asch (Prentice-Hall)
Little Duck. Dunn (Random House)
Little Kitten. Dunn (Random House)
Little Lamb. Dunn (Random House)
Little Rabbit. Dunn (Random House)
Pets in a Jar. Simon (Penguin)
Puppies Are Like That. Pfloog (Random House)
Snow Baby. Hillert (Caroline House)
Watching Foxes. Arnosky (Lothrop, Lee & Shepard)
What I Like About Toads. Howes (Harper & Row)
Wild Orphan Friends. Weber (Holt, Rinehart & Winston)

For Grown-ups

Pets and Animal Friends! is a picture book that introduces children to the care and characteristics of animals they are likely to know at home, at the zoo, or on a farm. Easy-to-read descriptions and special activities offer suggestions for participating in the animal world either by adopting and visiting animal friends or by reading and talking about them with adults and other children.

The editors invite interested adults to examine the sampling of reading level estimates below. Reading level estimates help adults decide what reading materials are appropriate for children at certain grade levels. These estimates are useful because they are usually based on syllable, word, and sentence counts — information that is taken from the text itself.

As useful as reading level scores are, however, we have not slavishly followed the dictates of readability formulas in our efforts to encourage young readers. Most reading specialists agree that reading skill is built on practice in reading, listening, speaking, and drawing meaning from language — activities that adults "do" when they read with children. These factors are not measured by readability scores; and yet they do enhance a text's value and appeal for children at early reading levels.

In *Pets and Animal Friends!*, the "Contents," "Things to Talk About," "Things to Do," index, and "More Books to Read About Pets and Animal Friends" sections help children become good readers by encouraging them to <u>use</u> the words they read as conveyors of meaning, not as objects to be memorized. And these sections give adults a chance to participate in the learning — and fun — to be found in this book.

Reading Level Analysis: SPACHE 3.3, FRY 3, FLESCH 92 (very easy), RAYGOR 3, FOG 6, SMOG 3